WRITE CHILDREN'S BOOKS : A GUIDE TO HELP YOU PUBLISH

First edition. May 1, 2024.

ISBN: 979-8224398072

Written by Kim Ruff-Moore.

Acknowledgments:

With deepest appreciation, I extend my heartfelt gratitude to everyone who has played a part in the creation of this book, "Write a Children's Book: A Guide to Help You Publish." Writing and publishing a book is a collaborative effort, and I am incredibly grateful for the support and encouragement of so many amazing individuals along the way.

First and foremost, I want to express my sincere thanks to my husband, Jeff, for his unwavering love, support, and encouragement throughout this journey. Your belief in me and your endless encouragement have been my greatest source of strength and inspiration.

I am also profoundly grateful to my family for their patience, understanding, and unwavering support as I pursued my passion for writing and publishing. Your love and encouragement have been my guiding light, and I am forever grateful for your presence in my life.

To my mentors, colleagues, and fellow authors, thank you for sharing your wisdom, insights, and expertise with me. Your guidance and encouragement have been invaluable, and I am grateful for the lessons I have learned from each of you.

A special thank you to the talented professionals who have contributed to the creation of this book—editors, designers, illustrators, and more. Your creativity, talent, and dedication to excellence have brought this project to life, and I am grateful for the opportunity to collaborate with such amazing individuals.

To my readers and supporters, thank you for embracing my work with enthusiasm and passion. Your feedback, reviews, and words of encouragement mean the world to me, and I am honored to share my passion for children's literature with you.

Last but not least, I want to express my gratitude to the countless authors, illustrators, publishers, and industry professionals who have inspired and influenced my journey as a writer and publisher. Your creativity, innovation, and dedication to storytelling continue to inspire me every day.

Thank you to each and every one of you for being a part of this incredible journey. Writing and publishing "Write a Children's Book" has been a dream come true, and I am grateful for the love and support that has made it possible.

With deepest appreciation,
Kim Ruff Moore

This book is dedicated to all Aspiring Authors who desire to write children's books.

Write Children's Books:
A Guide To Help You Publish

By Kim Ruff- Moore

Other Titles Available by Kim Ruff Moore:
Books for Adults:

- "Never Put All Your Eggs in One Basket"
- "Serendipity"
- "Cuffed"
- "Marriage Releases God's Favor"
- "Superheroes Teach"
- "I Speak Life"
- "I Speak Life Devotional"
- "Secrets of a Successful Published Author"
- "Jealousy Makes You Sick"
- "Waymaker"
- "Girl, Mash The Gas: Stop Procrastinating"
- "Girl, Forgive Them And Move On"

Children's Books:

- Suzzie Mocha Series
- Pavo the Parrot
- Otis the Brown Bear
- Kirby the Koala Series
- The Land of Unicorns Series
- Spence Seven Series
- Harper Sharper Series
- Sergio The Studio Mouse Series
- Piper The Pretty Pink Dinosaur Series

All titles are available at major book retailers including Books-A-Million, Walmart, Barnes and Noble, and Amazon, as well as other platforms. Visitwww.kimruffmoore.com[1] for more information and updates on new releases.

---

1. http://www.kimruffmoore.com/

Table of Contents:

Introduction

Writing a children's story is an exciting and rewarding journey. I remember watching a show that shared surprising statistics about the process of writing and publishing a book. It piqued my interest and set me on a path to become a children's author. At the beginning of my journey, excitement pulsed through me, but I also had many questions swirling in my mind. So, I delved into studying, watched numerous tutorials, and keenly listened to advice, absorbing every detail to avoid stumbling over common pitfalls. Cost considerations loomed large, and choices seemed endless. Yet, armed with determination, I persisted. Today, having published over 30 children's books across various series, I can confidently say that I've found my passion. It's a joyous ride, and the rewards are immense. In this book, I aim to lay out your options plainly and guide you through the process of publishing your own children's book. Surprisingly, while 81% of people express a desire to write a book, only 15% take the first step. Even fewer, a mere 6%, reach the halfway mark, and a mere 3% see their projects through to completion. But with the right guidance and determination, you can be among that 3%.

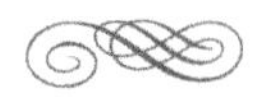

EMBARKING ON THE JOURNEY of writing and publishing a children's book requires dedication and perseverance. It's not just about having a great idea; it's about putting in the hard work to see it through. Along the way, you'll encounter challenges and uncertainties, but each hurdle is an opportunity to learn and grow. As you navigate the process, you'll need to make choices about everything from illustrations to printing options to marketing strategies.

However, don't let the daunting statistics deter you. Instead, let them inspire you to be part of the small percentage who turn their dreams into reality. With determination and the right resources, you can be one of the few who see their children's book come to life.

In this book, I'll share everything I've learned from my own experiences as a children's author. From crafting compelling stories to navigating the publishing industry, I'll provide practical advice and valuable insights to help you along your journey. Whether you're just starting out or struggling to finish your manuscript, I hope this book will serve as a beacon of guidance and encouragement.

So, if you've ever dreamed of writing a children's book, now is the time to take that first step. With passion as your fuel and perseverance as your compass, you can turn your dream into a published reality. Let's embark on this adventure together and bring your story to life for children to enjoy and cherish for years to come.

Writing a children's book is not just about storytelling; it's about creating magic on the page, capturing the imagination of young readers, and leaving a lasting impact. As you embark on this journey, remember that every word you write has the potential to inspire, educate, and entertain. Whether you're penning a whimsical tale of adventure or a heartfelt story of friendship, your voice matters.

Throughout this book, I'll share practical tips, resources, and advice to help you navigate the intricacies of the publishing world. From refining your manuscript to finding the right illustrator, from understanding the importance of cover design to marketing your book effectively, each chapter will equip you with the knowledge and tools you need to succeed.

But beyond the technical aspects, I'll also delve into the heart of storytelling. We'll explore the power of imagination, the joy of creativity, and the profound impact that children's literature can have on young minds. Because ultimately, writing a children's book is not just about reaching the finish line; it's about the journey of self-discovery, the joy of creation, and the privilege of sharing your story with the world.

So, whether you're a seasoned writer or a novice just starting out, I invite you to join me on this adventure. Let's embark on a journey of creativity, exploration, and discovery as we unlock the secrets to writing and publishing a children's book. Together, we'll bring your stories to life and inspire a new generation of readers.

Remember to stay true to your vision and embrace the unique voice that sets your story apart. Along the way, you may encounter setbacks and moments of doubt, but don't let them deter you. Instead, let them fuel your determination to persevere and see your project through to completion.

Your words have the power to resonate with young hearts and minds, sparking imagination and instilling lifelong lessons. So, take the time to craft your story with care, infusing it with authenticity, empathy, and wonder.

And as you navigate the publishing process, don't be afraid to seek support and guidance from fellow writers, mentors, and industry professionals. Building a network of like-minded individuals can provide invaluable insights and encouragement as you work towards your goals.

Above all, remember that writing a children's book is a labor of love. It's a journey filled with highs and lows, triumphs and challenges. But with passion as your compass and perseverance as your guide, you have the power to bring your dreams to life and share your stories with the world. So, take that first step, embrace the adventure that lies ahead, and let your imagination soar.

Discovering Your Story

When I set out to write a children's book, the first challenge I faced was finding the perfect story to tell. It's not always easy to pinpoint exactly what you want to write about, but I quickly learned that inspiration can be found in the most unexpected places. Sometimes it's a childhood memory that sparks an idea, or perhaps a conversation with a young reader that ignites your imagination.

To help you uncover your story, I've included exercises and prompts throughout this chapter designed to jumpstart your creativity. Whether it's brainstorming character traits or imagining new worlds, these activities are meant to get your creative juices flowing and help you develop your ideas further.

One thing I discovered along the way is that themes and messages play a crucial role in children's literature. Kids are perceptive, and they're drawn to stories that resonate with them on a deeper level. So as you explore different story ideas, consider what themes and messages you want to convey to your young readers. Whether it's the importance of friendship, the power of imagination, or the value of perseverance, finding themes that resonate can elevate your story and make it more meaningful to your audience.

Once you find out what you want to write about, you'll be surprised at how much easier the writing process becomes. Having a clear idea of your story's themes and messages will guide you as you craft your manuscript, making it easier to stay focused and on track. So take your time exploring different ideas, and don't be afraid to let your imagination run wild. After all, the best stories often come from the heart, and there's no limit to what you can create when you let your creativity soar.

As you delve deeper into the process of discovering your story, remember that inspiration can come from anywhere and everywhere. Keep your mind open to new experiences, observe the world around you with curiosity, and don't hesitate to jot down any ideas that come to mind, no matter how small or seemingly insignificant they may seem at the time.

The exercises and prompts included in this chapter are meant to be starting points, but don't feel constrained by them. Feel free to adapt and modify them to suit your own creative process. Whether you prefer to brainstorm with pen and paper, create vision boards, or engage in freewriting exercises, the key is to find what works best for you.

It's also important to trust in your instincts and follow your passion. If a particular story idea excites you and sparks joy, chances are it will resonate with young readers as well. Writing from a place of authenticity and passion will not only make the process more enjoyable for you but also make your story more compelling and relatable to your audience.

And remember, discovering your story is just the beginning of the journey. As you continue to develop your ideas and flesh out your characters and plot, don't be afraid to embrace the creative process fully. Allow yourself the freedom to explore new possibilities, take risks, and make mistakes along the way. After all, it's through these experiences that we grow as writers and storytellers.

So take a deep breath, trust in your creativity, and let the journey of discovering your story unfold. You never know what magical adventures await you on the pages of your children's book.

As I reflect on the journey that led me to become a children's author, I can't help but think back to the inspiration behind my very first book. It all began with memories of Easter, a holiday filled with joy and tradition from my childhood. Each year, my mother would lovingly prepare Easter baskets for my four sisters and me, along with new dresses and shoes. The night before Easter Sunday was always special, as my mother would skillfully straighten our hair with a hot comb, getting us all dolled up for the occasion.

But it wasn't just the material gifts that made Easter memorable; it was the traditions and rituals that brought our family together. We would attend church on Sunday morning, where we'd recite Easter speeches as part of the program. And after the service, we'd eagerly participate in an Easter egg hunt, scouring the church grounds for hidden treasures.

One vivid memory stands out among the rest: my mother, tirelessly coloring eggs and preparing deviled eggs and colorful cupcakes. Her dedication and love for our family shone brightly in those moments, and it's those memories that inspired my first children's book.

"Rosie and the Easter Egg Hunt" was born from those cherished memories, capturing the essence of joy, tradition, and family togetherness that I experienced as a child. In the book, Rosie not only enjoys the excitement of the Easter egg hunt but also discovers the value of friendship along the way. Through Rosie's adventures, young readers learn about patience, fun, and the importance of fostering meaningful connections with others.

From the initial spark of inspiration to the finished product, creating "Rosie and the Easter Egg Hunt" was a labor of love. I took on the challenge of illustrating the book myself, pouring my heart and soul into every page. And when it was finally published, I felt an immense sense of pride and accomplishment.

As I continue on my journey as a children's author, I carry with me the lessons learned from my first book. I've come to realize that inspiration can be found in the most ordinary of moments, and that storytelling is a powerful way to share our experiences and connect with others. So as you embark on your own journey of discovering your story, remember to cherish the memories that shape you, and let your imagination soar. Who knows what wonderful adventures await you on the pages of your own children's book?

Continuing on the path of my journey as a children's author, "Rosie and the Easter Egg Hunt" remains a cornerstone in my collection of works. The process of bringing Rosie's story to life was not only a labor of love but also a testament to the power of cherished memories and the enduring bonds of family.

As I embarked on the creation of "Rosie and the Easter Egg Hunt," I delved deep into my own childhood experiences, drawing upon the warmth and nostalgia of Easter celebrations with my family. Every stroke of the pen and brush was infused with the joy and love that filled those cherished moments, from the excitement of the egg hunt to the laughter shared with loved ones.

One of the most fulfilling aspects of creating this book was the opportunity to impart valuable lessons to young readers. Through Rosie's journey, children learn not only about the joy of Easter festivities but also about the importance of patience, friendship, and adventure. Rosie's interactions with her newfound friend serve as a reminder that the greatest treasures in life are often found in the connections we make with others.

As I reflect on the journey from inspiration to publication, I am filled with a profound sense of gratitude for the opportunity to share Rosie's story with the world. The positive feedback from readers has been immensely rewarding, reaffirming my belief in the transformative power of storytelling.

Moving forward, I am inspired to continue crafting stories that capture the imagination and touch the hearts of young readers everywhere. Each new book is an opportunity to explore new themes, characters, and adventures, and I am eager to see where this journey takes me next.

But no matter where my path as a children's author leads, "Rosie and the Easter Egg Hunt" will always hold a special place in my heart. It is a testament to the enduring power of love, family, and tradition, and a reminder that the greatest stories are often inspired by the moments that matter most.

Determine Your Target Age Audience

Determining your target age audience is a crucial step in crafting children's books, as it shapes everything from the complexity of the storyline to the tone and language used. For my books, I've chosen a target audience ranging from ages 3 to 7, with the understanding that older children up to around age 10 may still find enjoyment in them. This age range aligns with the magic and innocence of young readers, capturing a time in their lives when imagination knows no bounds and every story is an adventure waiting to unfold.

When writing for this age group, I aim to strike a delicate balance between simplicity and depth, ensuring that the themes and messages are accessible and engaging for young minds. I keep the length of my books relatively short, typically ranging from 24 to 36 pages, to maintain the attention span of young readers and allow for multiple readings in one sitting.

By focusing on this target age audience, I'm able to create stories that resonate with the unique experiences and interests of preschoolers and early elementary school children. Whether it's tales of friendship, exploration, or self-discovery, I strive to capture the wonder and curiosity that define this magical stage of childhood.

Ultimately, my goal is to preserve the innocence and magic of youth through my books, providing young readers with a gateway to imaginative worlds where anything is possible. By understanding and embracing the age-specific needs and interests of my target audience, I can create stories that not only entertain but also inspire, educate, and spark a lifelong love of reading.

While my current focus remains on creating children's books for the age range of 3 to 7, I'm open to the possibility of stretching myself and exploring new horizons in the future. As I continue to grow and evolve as a writer, I may decide to embark on projects targeting early teens and the age group right before that. Only time will tell where my creative journey will take me next.

Venturing into writing for older age groups presents exciting opportunities to delve into more complex themes, develop richer character arcs, and explore narratives that resonate with the experiences and challenges faced by preteens and young adolescents. It's a chance to expand my storytelling repertoire and connect with a broader audience of readers.

While the transition to writing for older age groups may require me to adapt my writing style and approach, I'm confident that the skills and insights I've gained from crafting children's books will serve as a strong foundation for this new endeavor. Whether it's crafting coming-of-age stories, exploring themes of identity and belonging, or tackling issues relevant to young adults, I'm eager to stretch myself creatively and explore new storytelling territories.

But for now, I remain committed to delighting and inspiring young readers with my children's books, nurturing their love of reading and imagination. As I continue on my journey as a writer, I look forward to whatever the future may hold, embracing new challenges and opportunities with enthusiasm and curiosity. Who knows what exciting adventures await in the pages of my next book? Only time will tell.

In the meantime, as I explore the possibility of writing for older age groups, I remain deeply rooted in my dedication to preserving the magic and innocence of childhood through my current children's books. There's something truly special about the wonder and joy that young readers experience when they immerse themselves in a captivating story, and I cherish the opportunity to be a part of that journey.

Each page I write is a testament to the boundless imagination and curiosity of children, and I take great pride in creating stories that ignite their sense of wonder and possibility. Whether it's a whimsical adventure through a magical forest or a heartwarming tale of friendship and kindness, my goal is to spark joy, inspire creativity, and instill valuable life lessons in young minds.

As I look ahead to the future, I remain grateful for the support and enthusiasm of readers who have embraced my children's books with open hearts and eager minds. It's their encouragement and feedback that motivates me to continue pushing the boundaries of my creativity and exploring new avenues of storytelling.

So, while I may one day venture into writing for older age groups, my commitment to crafting enchanting and meaningful children's books remains unwavering. After all, there's no greater joy than seeing the smile on a child's face as they lose themselves in the pages of a good book. And for me, that's the greatest reward of all.

Benefits Of Creating A Book Series

The power of a captivating book series cannot be overstated, and examples from beloved authors like J.K. Rowling to iconic characters like Junie B. Jones and Diary of a Wimpy Kid demonstrate the enduring appeal and impact of a well-crafted series.

One of the key benefits of a book series is the opportunity for readers to become deeply invested in the characters, worlds, and storylines over the course of multiple books. By immersing themselves in the rich tapestry of a series, readers develop a sense of familiarity and connection with the characters, allowing them to form emotional attachments and experience a deeper level of engagement with the story. Whether it's following the adventures of Harry Potter at Hogwarts, navigating the antics of Junie B. Jones in elementary school, or exploring the hilarious misadventures of Greg Heffley in middle school, readers are drawn into the lives of these characters and eagerly anticipate each new installment in their journey.

Furthermore, a book series allows authors to explore complex narratives and character arcs in greater depth than would be possible in a standalone novel. By unfolding the story over multiple books, authors have the opportunity to delve into deeper themes, introduce new plot twists, and develop the characters in meaningful and surprising ways. This depth and complexity not only enriches the reading experience for fans but also keeps them eagerly turning the pages in anticipation of what will happen next.

Moreover, a successful book series can create a sense of community and camaraderie among fans who share a common love for the characters and world of the story. Whether it's discussing theories, sharing fan art, or attending book-related events and conventions, readers of a series often form tight-knit communities that celebrate their shared passion for the books. This sense of belonging and connection adds an additional layer of enjoyment to the reading experience and fosters a sense of belonging and connection among fans.

Additionally, from a business perspective, a book series can be incredibly lucrative for authors and publishers alike. Once a series gains momentum and a loyal fan base, each new installment becomes a highly anticipated event, driving sales and generating buzz in the literary world. Merchandising opportunities, such as toys, games, and movie adaptations, can further expand the reach and profitability of a successful series, turning it into a multimedia phenomenon with lasting cultural impact.

The benefits of a good book series are manifold, from deepening reader engagement and emotional investment to fostering a sense of community and generating commercial success. Whether it's exploring the magical world of Hogwarts, the zany adventures of a precocious kindergartener, or the hilarious escapades of a middle schooler, a well-crafted series has the power to captivate readers of all ages and leave a lasting impression on their hearts and minds. So here's to the joy of discovering new worlds, embarking on epic adventures, and celebrating the enduring magic of a beloved book series.

Certainly! Let's explore the exciting possibilities that television adaptations offer for successful book series:

Television adaptations of popular book series have become increasingly prevalent in recent years, offering fans a new way to experience their favorite stories and characters on the small screen. From beloved classics like "Harry Potter" and "Percy Jackson" to contemporary hits like "Game of Thrones" television adaptations have the power to bring the richly imagined worlds of books to life in vivid detail, captivating audiences with compelling storytelling, memorable characters, and breathtaking visuals.

One of the key benefits of television adaptations is the opportunity to explore the expansive narratives and complex character arcs of book series in greater depth than would be possible in a single film. By unfolding the story over multiple episodes or seasons, television adaptations can delve into the intricacies of the plot, develop secondary characters, and explore subplots and themes that may have been overlooked in the original source material. This allows for a more immersive and comprehensive storytelling experience that resonates with both existing fans and new audiences alike.

Television adaptations have the potential to reach a wider audience than books alone, as they can be broadcast or streamed to millions of viewers around the world. This increased visibility not only introduces the story to new fans but also fosters a sense of community and shared experience among viewers who come together to discuss and dissect each episode. Television adaptations can also generate renewed interest in the original books, driving book sales and expanding the fan base even further.

Furthermore, television adaptations offer authors and creators the opportunity to collaborate with talented writers, directors, and actors to bring their vision to life on screen. By partnering with experienced professionals in the television industry, authors can ensure that their stories are translated faithfully and respectfully to the screen while also benefiting from fresh perspectives and creative interpretations that enhance the viewing experience for audiences.

Additionally, television adaptations can open up exciting opportunities for expanded storytelling, such as spin-off series, prequels, or companion shows that explore different aspects of the fictional universe. By expanding the scope of the narrative beyond the confines of the original books, television adaptations can satisfy fans' curiosity and offer new insights into beloved characters and settings. This can create a rich blend of interconnected stories and experiences that enrich the overall viewing experience and keep audiences engaged for years to come.

Television adaptations offer a wealth of exciting possibilities for successful book series, from deepening the storytelling and character development to reaching new audiences and expanding the fictional universe. Whether it's bringing iconic characters to life, exploring new storylines, or delving into the intricacies of a beloved world, television adaptations have the power to captivate viewers and leave a lasting impression on the cultural landscape. So here's to the magic of television adaptations and the endless possibilities they hold for bringing the worlds of books to life on screen.

Television adaptations can provide authors and creators with the opportunity to explore narrative avenues that may not have been feasible in the original books. With the extended runtime of a television series, there is more room to delve into character backstories, introduce new plotlines, and explore the nuances of the fictional world in greater detail. This creative freedom allows authors to expand upon their original vision and offer fans a fresh perspective on familiar stories and characters.

Additionally, television adaptations can breathe new life into beloved book series by reimagining them for a modern audience. By updating the setting, themes, and tone to reflect contemporary sensibilities, television adaptations can resonate with viewers in ways that feel relevant and relatable. This can attract a new generation of fans while also appealing to longtime readers who are eager to see their favorite stories brought to life in a fresh and exciting way.

Television adaptations can serve as a platform for diverse representation and inclusivity, allowing authors and creators to showcase a wide range of voices, perspectives, and experiences on screen. By casting actors from diverse backgrounds, exploring diverse cultures and identities, and addressing social issues with sensitivity and authenticity, television adaptations can promote greater understanding, empathy, and acceptance among viewers of all ages. This commitment to diversity and representation not only enriches the storytelling but also reflects the diversity of the real world and the experiences of real people.

Furthermore, television adaptations can provide authors with a valuable opportunity to engage with their fans in new and meaningful ways. By participating in interviews, behind-the-scenes features, and social media campaigns, authors can connect with viewers on a personal level and share insights into their creative process, inspirations, and vision for the series. This interaction fosters a sense of community and collaboration between authors and fans, creating a shared experience that extends beyond the pages of the book or the screen of the television.

Also I've noticed, television adaptations can generate lucrative opportunities for authors and creators through licensing and merchandising deals. From action figures and apparel to video games and theme park attractions, the potential for merchandise tie-ins and brand extensions is virtually limitless. By leveraging the popularity of the television series, authors can expand their brand and generate additional revenue streams that enhance their overall success and visibility in the marketplace.

At the end of the day, television adaptations offer a wealth of opportunities for authors and creators to expand upon their original vision, reach new audiences, and engage with fans in exciting and innovative ways. Whether it's exploring new narrative avenues, promoting diversity and inclusivity, or capitalizing on merchandising opportunities, television adaptations have the power to elevate beloved book series to new heights of success and cultural relevance. So here's to the magic of television adaptations and the endless possibilities they hold for bringing the worlds of books to life on screen.

Illustrating Compelling Characters

When it comes to writing a children's book, creating characters that resonate with your audience is essential. But for many aspiring authors, including myself, this can be a daunting task. How do you breathe life into your characters and make them leap off the page? It's a question I've grappled with countless times.

I've developed techniques and strategies that have helped me craft memorable and relatable characters.

The key to creating compelling characters lies in understanding their motivations, quirks, and flaws. Just like real people, fictional characters should have depth and complexity that readers can connect with. One technique I use is to develop detailed character profiles, outlining their personalities, backgrounds, and goals. This helps me get inside their heads and understand what makes them tick.

But crafting compelling characters isn't just about fleshing out their traits; it's also about giving them compelling arcs and growth throughout the story. Whether it's overcoming obstacles, facing their fears, or learning valuable lessons, characters should evolve and change over the course of the narrative. This not only adds depth to the story but also keeps readers engaged and invested in their journey.

Another crucial aspect of creating compelling characters is writing authentic and engaging dialogue. Dialogue is a powerful tool for revealing character traits, relationships, and emotions. To make dialogue feel natural and believable, I often read it aloud or imagine myself in the character's shoes. This helps me capture their unique voice and personality, making the interactions between characters feel genuine and dynamic.

Now, when it comes to illustrating my own books, I've found that having control over the visual elements allows me to bring my characters to life in exactly the way I envision them. However, I understand that not everyone has this ability, and outsourcing illustrations can be both costly and time-consuming.

If you find yourself in need of illustration help, it's essential to establish clear expectations and agreements with whoever you choose to work with. I approach this process much like I do with my music, using a "contract for hire" to outline specific terms, including deadlines, fees, and copyright language. Having a clear contract not only protects your interests but also ensures that both parties are on the same page throughout the creative process.

Ultimately, crafting compelling characters is both an art and a science. It requires creativity, empathy, and attention to detail. But by following these techniques and strategies, you can create characters that resonate with your audience and bring your story to life in vibrant and unforgettable ways.

Even if you're collaborating with a friend or family member on illustrating your book, it's crucial to have a contract in place to protect your intellectual property and clarify expectations. While it may feel uncomfortable to formalize agreements with loved ones, having a clear contract ensures that both parties understand their roles, rights, and responsibilities. As the creator of the manuscript, it's important to safeguard your work and ensure that your vision is accurately represented in the illustrations. By outlining specifics such as deadlines, fees, copyright ownership, and any potential consequences for breach of contract, you can mitigate misunderstandings and conflicts down the line. Remember, a well-drafted contract not only protects your interests but also fosters a professional and respectful working relationship with your collaborator.

On my journey as a children's author, I've found that using stock illustrations can be a valuable alternative, especially if you're not skilled in illustration or if hiring an illustrator isn't feasible. Stock illustrations offer a wide range of pre-made artwork that you can customize to fit your vision perfectly. This flexibility allows me to bring my characters and scenes to life exactly as I envision them, without the constraints of my own artistic abilities or the limitations of a hired illustrator's style.

With stock illustrations, I have access to a vast library of high-quality images, spanning different genres, themes, and styles. Whether I'm writing a whimsical fairy tale or a contemporary adventure, I can easily find illustrations that complement my story and enhance its visual appeal. And because stock illustrations are readily available for purchase, I can save time and resources compared to commissioning custom artwork.

Using stock illustrations also grants me full creative control over my projects. I can mix and match elements, adjust colors and compositions, and experiment with different layouts until I achieve the perfect look for my book. This level of autonomy allows me to stay true to my vision and bring my stories to life in a way that feels authentic and unique.

Overall, incorporating stock illustrations into my work has been a game-changer, offering me the flexibility, affordability, and creative freedom I need to create engaging and visually stunning children's books. Whether you're an experienced author or just starting out, exploring the world of stock illustrations can open up a world of possibilities for bringing your stories to life in vibrant and imaginative ways.

One of the most rewarding aspects of creating characters is watching them evolve over the course of the story. I've found that giving characters room to grow and change allows them to resonate more deeply with readers. Whether it's a shy protagonist finding their voice or a mischievous sidekick learning the value of friendship, character arcs add richness and depth to the narrative.

In addition to character growth, authentic dialogue plays a crucial role in bringing characters to life. Dialogue not only moves the plot forward but also reveals important facets of each character's personality, relationships, and motivations. To ensure that dialogue feels genuine and engaging, I often draw inspiration from real-life conversations and observations. Listening to the cadence and rhythm of speech helps me capture the unique voices of my characters and create dialogue that rings true.

While I take pride in illustrating my own books, I recognize that not everyone has the same skill set or resources. Outsourcing illustrations can be a viable option, but it comes with its own set of challenges. Finding the right illustrator who can bring your vision to life while staying within budget and meeting deadlines can be a daunting task. That's why establishing clear expectations and agreements from the outset is essential. A well-defined contract not only protects both parties but also ensures a smooth and collaborative process from start to finish.

As I continue on my journey as a children's author, I remain committed to honing my craft and creating characters that inspire, entertain, and resonate with young readers. Each new book presents its own set of challenges and opportunities, but through dedication, creativity, and collaboration, I'm confident that I can bring my characters and stories to life in ways that captivate and delight audiences of all ages.

The Odds Are Stacked Against You

The odds of getting a children's book published through traditional means, such as securing a deal with a traditional publishing house or literary agent, can indeed seem daunting. With acceptance rates estimated to be between 1% and 2% in the industry, many aspiring authors face significant challenges in getting their work noticed and accepted by traditional publishers. However, it's essential to understand the factors that contribute to these odds and the alternatives available to authors who are determined to see their children's books in print.

One of the primary reasons for the low acceptance rates in traditional publishing is the sheer volume of manuscripts received by publishers and literary agents on a daily basis. With countless aspiring authors vying for limited slots on publishers' lists, competition is fierce, and only the most exceptional manuscripts stand a chance of being selected for publication. This high level of competition means that publishers and agents can afford to be extremely selective in their acquisitions, often favoring established authors or manuscripts that are deemed to have significant commercial potential.

Furthermore, the subjective nature of the publishing industry means that what one editor or agent may love, another may pass on. This can make it challenging for authors to predict which manuscripts will resonate with publishing professionals and ultimately find a home with a traditional publisher. Additionally, factors such as market trends, genre preferences, and the individual tastes of editors and agents can all influence the likelihood of a manuscript being accepted for publication.

Moreover, traditional publishers typically invest significant time and resources into the editorial, design, production, marketing, and distribution aspects of publishing a book. As a result, they are often seeking manuscripts that not only demonstrate exceptional writing and storytelling but also have the potential to appeal to a broad audience and generate substantial sales. This means that manuscripts that are deemed too niche, experimental, or unconventional may struggle to find a home with traditional publishers, further reducing the odds of acceptance for aspiring authors.

Given these challenges, many authors are turning to alternative publishing options, such as self-publishing and independent publishing, as a way to bypass the traditional gatekeepers of the industry and bring their children's books directly to readers. Self-publishing, in particular, has become increasingly popular in recent years, thanks to advances in technology and the rise of online platforms that enable authors to publish and distribute their books with minimal upfront costs and maximum creative control.

Self-publishing allows authors to retain full ownership and control over their work, from the writing and editing process to the design, production, and marketing stages. This means that authors can publish their books on their own terms, without having to compromise their vision or artistic integrity to meet the demands of traditional publishers. Additionally, self-publishing offers authors the flexibility to experiment with different formats, genres, and distribution channels, allowing them to tailor their publishing strategy to their specific goals and target audience.

Independent publishing, on the other hand, offers authors the opportunity to work with small presses or boutique publishing houses that specialize in niche markets or genres. While independent publishers may not have the same resources or reach as traditional publishing houses, they often offer authors a more personalized and collaborative publishing experience, with greater attention to detail and a focus on building long-term relationships with their authors.

Ultimately, whether an author chooses to pursue traditional publishing, self-publishing, or independent publishing depends on their individual goals, preferences, and priorities. While the odds of getting a children's book published through traditional means may be low, there are plenty of alternative paths to publication available to authors who are willing to explore them. With determination, perseverance, and a willingness to think outside the box, aspiring authors can increase their chances of seeing their children's books in print and sharing their stories with the world.

Indeed, while independent publishing offers authors an alternative route to traditional publishing, the challenges of bringing a children's book to market remain significant. Despite the freedom and flexibility that self-publishing and independent publishing provide, aspiring authors still face considerable hurdles on the path to successfully launching their books.

One of the primary challenges authors encounter in independent publishing is the sheer volume of manuscripts that flood the market. With the barriers to entry significantly lower than in traditional publishing, the number of self-published and independently published books has exploded in recent years. As a result, the market is saturated with a vast array of titles, making it increasingly difficult for individual books to stand out and gain traction with readers.

Furthermore, the rise of self-publishing platforms and print-on-demand services has democratized the publishing process, allowing anyone with a story to tell to bring their book to market. While this accessibility is a boon for aspiring authors, it also means that the quality and professionalism of independently published books can vary widely. With so many titles competing for readers' attention, authors must invest significant time and effort into ensuring that their books are of the highest quality in terms of writing, editing, design, and production.

Moreover, the challenges of marketing and promoting independently published books cannot be overstated. Unlike traditional publishing houses, which have dedicated marketing and publicity teams to support their authors, independent authors are responsible for promoting their books themselves. This often requires authors to become proficient in a wide range of skills, from social media marketing and email outreach to book signings and author events. Navigating the complex landscape of book marketing can be daunting, particularly for authors who are new to the industry or lack experience in self-promotion.

Additionally, the financial realities of independent publishing can be prohibitive for many aspiring authors. While self-publishing eliminates the need to secure a publishing deal or literary agent, authors must still invest in professional editing, cover design, formatting, printing, and distribution services to produce a high-quality book. These costs can quickly add up, and authors may struggle to recoup their investment if their books fail to gain traction in the competitive marketplace.

Despite these challenges, many authors are drawn to independent publishing by the promise of creative freedom, control over their work, and the potential for higher royalties. By taking ownership of the publishing process and embracing the entrepreneurial mindset, authors can navigate the complexities of independent publishing and increase their chances of success. This may involve investing in professional services, building a strong author platform, cultivating a loyal readership, and continually refining their marketing and promotional strategies.

While independent publishing offers authors an alternative path to traditional publishing, the road to success is not without its obstacles. From standing out in a crowded marketplace to mastering the intricacies of book marketing and promotion, aspiring authors face numerous challenges on the journey to independently publishing their children's books. However, with determination, resilience, and a commitment to excellence, authors can overcome these challenges and achieve their dreams of bringing their stories to life for readers to enjoy.

Additionally, the journey of independent publishing for children's books is further complicated by the unique considerations and requirements of the genre. Children's books often involve intricate illustrations, engaging storytelling, and age-appropriate content that must resonate with young readers and their caregivers. As a result, independent authors must not only master the craft of writing but also collaborate closely with illustrators, editors, and designers to create a polished and professional product that meets the high standards of the children's publishing industry.

Furthermore, children's books require careful attention to detail in terms of content, format, and presentation to ensure that they are developmentally appropriate and appealing to their target audience. From selecting the right themes and language to crafting engaging characters and storylines, authors must strike the delicate balance between entertaining and educating young readers while also adhering to the expectations of parents, educators, and librarians. This requires a deep understanding of child development, literacy skills, and educational principles, as well as a willingness to engage with feedback and adapt the content accordingly.

Moreover, the distribution and discoverability of independently published children's books can pose significant challenges for authors seeking to reach their target audience. While online platforms such as

Amazon, Barnes & Noble, and Apple Books offer convenient channels for selling and distributing books, authors must compete with a vast array of titles for visibility and sales. Without the marketing and promotional support of a traditional publisher, independent authors must rely on grassroots efforts, word-of-mouth recommendations, and strategic partnerships to increase awareness of their books and attract readers.

Additionally, the issue of credibility and legitimacy can be a concern for independent authors seeking to establish themselves in the children's publishing industry. While self-publishing has become increasingly accepted and respected in recent years, some readers, educators, and industry professionals may still harbor biases against independently published books, viewing them as inferior to traditionally published titles. Overcoming these preconceptions and building trust with readers and gatekeepers requires authors to consistently produce high-quality books, engage with their audience authentically, and actively participate in the broader children's literary community.

Despite these challenges, independent publishing offers authors a unique opportunity to bring their creative vision to life and connect directly with readers who are hungry for fresh and diverse voices in children's literature. By embracing the entrepreneurial spirit, leveraging digital tools and platforms, and fostering a supportive network of collaborators and readers, independent authors can navigate the complexities of publishing and carve out their own path to success in the competitive children's book market.

While the odds may be stacked against aspiring authors in the children's publishing industry, independent publishing offers a viable alternative for those who are willing to embrace the challenges and opportunities it presents. With determination, creativity, and a commitment to excellence, independent authors can overcome the obstacles of publishing and share their stories with the world, enriching the lives of young readers and shaping the future of children's literature for generations to come.

The percentage of people who choose to publish independently varies depending on the source and the specific criteria used to define independent publishing. However, it's generally agreed upon that a significant and growing number of authors are turning to self-publishing and independent publishing as viable alternatives to traditional publishing.

According to some industry estimates, self-published and independently published books now account for a substantial portion of overall book sales in the market. While exact figures can be difficult to pin down due to the decentralized nature of self-publishing platforms and the lack of centralized tracking mechanisms, studies suggest that independent authors collectively publish tens of thousands of new titles each year across a wide range of genres and categories.

One survey conducted by Bowker, the official ISBN agency for the United States, found that self-published titles accounted for approximately 30% of all ebook sales and 13% of all print book sales in the U.S. market in 2018. These figures indicate a significant and growing presence of independently published books in the marketplace, reflecting the increasing popularity and acceptance of self-publishing among authors and readers alike.

Furthermore, platforms like Amazon Kindle Direct Publishing (KDP), Smashwords, and IngramSpark have democratized the publishing process, allowing authors to publish and distribute their books with minimal upfront costs and maximum creative control. This accessibility has empowered countless authors to bring their stories to readers around the world, bypassing the traditional gatekeepers of the publishing industry and reaching audiences directly.

Despite the rise of independent publishing, however, it's important to acknowledge that the vast majority of self-published books do not achieve commercial success or widespread recognition. Many independently published authors struggle to attract readers, generate sales, and break through the noise of the crowded marketplace. Factors such as poor quality, lack of marketing and promotion, and limited distribution channels can all contribute to the challenges faced by independent authors in gaining visibility and traction for their books.

Additionally, while independent publishing offers authors greater freedom and control over their work, it also requires a significant investment of time, effort, and resources to produce a high-quality book and effectively market it to readers. Authors who choose to self-publish or independently publish must be prepared to wear multiple hats, serving as writer, editor, designer, marketer, and entrepreneur all at once.

While the percentage of people who publish independently is difficult to quantify precisely, there is no denying the significant and growing impact of self-publishing and independent publishing in the book industry. Aspiring authors who choose to take the independent route have access to unprecedented opportunities for creative expression and entrepreneurial success, but they must also be prepared to navigate the challenges and complexities of the publishing landscape with determination, resilience, and a commitment to excellence.

Navigating The Publishing Process

Navigating the publishing process for children's books can be a daunting task, but understanding your options and weighing the pros and cons can help you immensely. When I first embarked on this journey, I felt overwhelmed by the sheer number of choices available, from traditional publishing to self-publishing and hybrid publishing. Each path has its own advantages and challenges, and it's essential to do your research to determine which option aligns best with your goals and priorities.

Traditional publishing, for example, offers the prestige of working with established publishing houses, which can provide access to professional editing, design, and marketing services. However, securing a traditional publishing deal can be highly competitive, requiring patience, persistence, and a strong query letter or book proposal. Researching literary agents who specialize in children's literature and crafting a compelling query letter are essential steps in this process.

On the other hand, self-publishing empowers authors to retain full creative control over their books and keep a larger percentage of the profits. With the rise of print-on-demand and ebook distribution platforms, self-publishing has become more accessible than ever before. However, self-publishing also requires authors to take on additional responsibilities, such as editing, formatting, and marketing their books. It's crucial to approach self-publishing with a clear plan and realistic expectations to ensure success.

Hybrid publishing offers a middle ground between traditional publishing and self-publishing, providing authors with some of the benefits of both models. Hybrid publishers typically offer professional editing, design, and distribution services while allowing authors to retain more control over their books than traditional publishers. However, it's essential to research hybrid publishers carefully and ensure that they have a track record of success and transparency.

Regardless of which publishing path you choose, preparing your manuscript for submission or self-publishing is a crucial step in the process. This involves thorough editing and proofreading to ensure that your book is polished and error-free. You may also need to format your manuscript according to the requirements of your chosen publishing platform or prepare supplementary materials such as a synopsis or author bio.

In my own journey, I found valuable resources and insights by watching YouTube tutorials and seeking advice from fellow authors who had navigated the publishing process before me. These resources helped me understand the intricacies of the industry and make informed decisions about my publishing options. By taking the time to research and educate yourself, you can navigate the publishing process with confidence and clarity, bringing your children's book to life for readers to enjoy.

Traditional publishing can indeed feel like winning a major accolade, akin to being drafted into the NBA or winning a Grammy. It carries with it a sense of validation and prestige, as well as the potential for broader distribution and recognition. However, the process of securing a traditional publishing deal can be arduous and complex.

To begin the traditional publishing journey, authors typically need to have a polished manuscript that meets the standards of the publishing industry. This often involves multiple rounds of editing and revision to ensure that the book is of the highest quality. Once the manuscript is ready, authors then need to find a literary agent who will represent them and pitch their book to publishers on their behalf.

Finding the right literary agent can be a challenging task in itself, as agents receive countless submissions and have specific criteria for the books they choose to represent. Crafting a compelling query letter that grabs the agent's attention is essential, as it serves as the author's first introduction to potential representation.

If an agent is successful in securing a publishing deal for the author, the process is far from over. Traditional publishing contracts typically involve giving up a significant portion of the rights to the book, including copyright and distribution rights. Authors may also have limited control over the payment schedule, with advances and royalties often paid out in increments over time.

While some authors receive substantial advances upfront, others may receive more modest sums, or even none at all. Additionally, the payment schedule can be staggered, with authors receiving portions of their advance upon signing the contract, upon completion of manuscript revisions, and upon publication, among other milestones.

Despite these challenges, traditional publishers often provide valuable support in terms of marketing, distribution, and promotion. However, it's important to remember that publishers have a vested interest in the success of the books they choose to publish, as they stand to benefit from sales and royalties over the lifetime of the book.

Ultimately, the decision to pursue traditional publishing requires careful consideration of the pros and cons, as well as an understanding of the industry landscape. While traditional publishing offers certain advantages, such as access to professional editing and marketing services, it also comes with trade-offs in terms of rights, control, and financial compensation. As with any publishing path, it's essential for authors to weigh their options and choose the path that aligns best with their goals and priorities as writers.

For many authors, the allure of traditional publishing is undeniable, with its promise of prestige, editorial support, and wider distribution channels. However, it's essential to acknowledge the potential drawbacks and complexities involved in this route.

One of the most significant challenges of traditional publishing is the lengthy and often uncertain process of securing a publishing deal. As I've learned from industry insiders, including a young lady who worked for major publishing houses like Penguin and Random House, the journey from manuscript submission to bookshelf can be fraught with waiting periods and setbacks. Publishers receive countless submissions, and competition for limited slots on their publishing lists can be fierce. As a result, authors may face long waiting times for responses, or even multiple rejections before finding the right fit.

Moreover, traditional publishing contracts typically require authors to relinquish a significant portion of their rights to the book, including copyright and control over various aspects of the publishing process.

While this arrangement may provide access to professional editing, design, and marketing services, it also means that authors have less autonomy and ownership over their work. Payment schedules can also be fragmented, with advances and royalties dispersed over time, and the amounts offered may vary widely depending on factors such as market trends and perceived commercial potential.

Despite these challenges, traditional publishing remains a viable and respected path for many authors, offering opportunities for recognition, visibility, and support from industry professionals. However, it's crucial for authors to approach this route with realistic expectations and a clear understanding of the terms and conditions involved.

For those who value creative control, autonomy, and faster time-to-market, alternative publishing options such as self-publishing or hybrid publishing may be worth considering. These routes allow authors to retain greater control over their work, keep a larger share of the profits, and have more flexibility in terms of production timelines and distribution strategies.

Ultimately, the decision of which publishing path to pursue depends on a variety of factors, including individual goals, preferences, and resources. By carefully weighing the pros and cons of each option and seeking guidance from industry professionals, authors can make informed decisions that best serve their creative vision and career aspirations.

For me, the decision to take the independent route was a natural choice. However, instead of simply self-publishing, I opted to establish my own publishing company alongside my husband. As professional recording artists and singer-songwriters with a wealth of creative works, including original music, we recognized the importance of having a dedicated platform to showcase all of our artistic endeavors. Thus, Ruff Moore Media Publishing was born.

Creating our own publishing imprint allowed us to maintain complete creative control over our books, music, and other creative projects. We were no longer beholden to the constraints and limitations imposed by traditional publishing houses. Instead, we had the freedom to bring our vision to life on our own terms, without compromise.

One of the most significant advantages of establishing our own publishing company was the ability to build a brand that reflected our values, aesthetic, and creative ethos. From the logo design to the website layout, every aspect of our imprint was carefully crafted to resonate with our target audience and convey the essence of who we are as artists.

Moreover, having our own publishing company empowered us to take charge of every aspect of the publishing process, from manuscript editing to cover design to distribution. We were able to collaborate with trusted professionals and assemble a team that shared our vision and passion for storytelling.

Of course, with great power comes great responsibility, and we quickly realized that the success of our books ultimately rested on our shoulders. Unlike traditional publishing, where marketing and promotion are handled by the publisher, the onus was now on us to get the word out and connect with readers.

Despite the challenges of DIY marketing, we embraced the opportunity to engage directly with our audience and cultivate a loyal fanbase. From social media campaigns to book signings to virtual events, we explored a variety of strategies to raise awareness and generate buzz around our books.

Looking back, I'm grateful that we made the decision to establish our own publishing company. It has been a rewarding and fulfilling journey, allowing us to pursue our creative passions with autonomy and authenticity. And while the road may have been filled with twists and turns, I wouldn't have it any other way. Ruff Moore Media Publishing has become more than just a platform for our creative works; it's a labor of love and a testament to the power of following yAs we embarked on our journey with Ruff Moore Media Publishing, we quickly realized that the path of independent publishing came with its own set of challenges and opportunities. One of the most significant advantages was the freedom to experiment and innovate in our approach to marketing and promotion.

Without the constraints of traditional publishing contracts or corporate oversight, we had the flexibility to explore unconventional marketing tactics and connect with readers in unique ways. From organizing themed book events to collaborating with local businesses for cross-promotion, we embraced creativity and resourcefulness in our marketing efforts.

One strategy that proved particularly effective was leveraging our background as recording artists to cross-promote our books and music. We found that our existing fanbase was eager to support our literary endeavors, and vice versa. By incorporating elements of storytelling into our music and vice versa, we were able to create a cohesive brand identity that resonated with our audience across multiple platforms.

Another key aspect of our independent publishing journey was the emphasis on community building and grassroots engagement. We recognized the importance of fostering meaningful connections with readers, fellow authors, and industry professionals. Through social media engagement, networking events, and participation in local book fairs and festivals, we worked tirelessly to cultivate a supportive and engaged community around our brand.

Of course, navigating the world of independent publishing was not without its challenges. From logistical hurdles such as distribution and inventory management to the ongoing demands of self-promotion and marketing, we faced a steep learning curve along the way. However, each obstacle served as an opportunity for growth and learning, strengthening our resolve and deepening our commitment to our craft.

Despite the challenges, the rewards of independent publishing far outweighed the drawbacks. We found fulfillment in the creative freedom, autonomy, and sense of ownership that came with running our own publishing company. And while the journey may have been marked by ups and downs, we wouldn't trade it for anything.

Looking ahead, we remain excited about the possibilities that lie ahead for Ruff Moore Media Publishing. With each new book release, we continue to push the boundaries of our creativity, connect with readers, and build a legacy that reflects our passion for storytelling and artistic expression. And as we embark on the next chapter of our publishing journey, we do so with gratitude, determination, and an unwavering belief in the power of independent publishing to transform lives and inspire imaginations.

How Will You Publish

If you're considering how to publish your children's book, there are several routes to explore. Traditional publishing offers the prestige of working with established houses, but it can involve lengthy processes and giving up some creative control. Independent publishing grants you autonomy but requires handling everything from editing to marketing. Creating your own imprint gives you middle ground, with control and support. Whichever path you choose, ensuring accurate metadata, obtaining an ISBN, and securing wide distribution are crucial. Take time to weigh your options, considering your goals and resources, to make the best decision for your book and your author journey.

Once you've decided on your publishing route, it's time to dive into the nitty-gritty details. For traditional publishing, research literary agents who specialize in children's literature and craft a compelling query letter. If you're pursuing independent publishing, invest in professional editing and design services to ensure your book meets industry standards. Consider platforms like Barnes and Noble, Google play, Apple, Amazon Kindle Direct Publishing, Draft2digital or IngramSpark for distribution. If you're creating your own imprint, develop a strong brand identity and marketing strategy to distinguish your books in the marketplace. Remember to pay close attention to metadata accuracy, obtain an ISBN, and explore distribution options to reach your target audience effectively. With careful planning and attention to detail, you'll be well on your way to bringing your children's book to life.

It is essential to navigate the publishing process successfully and bring your children's book to eager young readers worldwide.

Once you've embarked on your chosen publishing path and begun the journey of bringing your children's book to life, it's essential to remain flexible and adaptive. Embrace the feedback and guidance provided by literary agents, editors, and other industry professionals if you're pursuing traditional publishing. For independent publishing, stay open to refining your approach based on market trends and reader feedback. Continuously monitor your marketing efforts and adjust strategies as needed to maximize visibility and engagement.

If you've decided to establish your own imprint, focus on fostering a strong community around your brand and books. Engage with readers through social media, author events, and other promotional activities to build a loyal fan base. Keep an eye on emerging technologies and distribution channels to stay ahead of the curve and reach new audiences effectively.

Throughout the publishing process, prioritize quality and professionalism in every aspect, from editing and design to marketing and distribution. Ensure that your book meets industry standards and stands out amidst the competition. By maintaining a high standard of excellence and remaining dedicated to your vision, you can successfully navigate the complexities of the publishing world and bring your children's book to fruition.

Remember that the journey doesn't end with publication—continue to nurture your book and career as an author by seeking opportunities for growth and expansion. Whether it's through sequels, spin-offs, or new projects, keep pushing boundaries and exploring new avenues for creativity and storytelling. With passion, perseverance, and a commitment to continuous improvement, you can achieve your goals and leave a lasting impact on young readers everywhere.

Preparing For Take Off

Okay for self-publishing, whether independently or through your own imprint, means taking on a multitude of tasks to ensure your book is ready for launch. Here's a detailed checklist to guide you through the process:

1. Manuscript Review: Ensure your manuscript is error-free, well-written, and engaging. If your book includes illustrations, make sure they are of high quality and enhance the storytelling.
2. Book Cover Design: Invest in a professional and eye-catching book cover design. This is the first impression readers will have of your book, so it needs to be competitive and of excellent quality.
3. Correct Book Format: Ensure your manuscript is formatted correctly for book printing or ebook conversion. Each platform may have specific requirements for trim size, page layout, and formatting.
4. ISBN Acquisition: Decide whether to use a free ISBN provided by publishing platforms like Amazon, or purchase your own ISBN for greater control and flexibility in publishing options.
5. Platform Selection: Research different publishing platforms such as Amazon Kindle Direct Publishing, IngramSpark, or Lulu. Each platform may offer different services, royalties, and distribution options.
6. Formatting for Each Platform: Understand the formatting requirements for each platform, including trim size, page layout, and cover specifications. Most platforms provide guidelines or templates to assist with formatting.
7. Book Description: Craft a powerful and concise book description that captures the essence of your story and entices readers to learn more.

8. Author Bio and Photo: Prepare a compelling author bio and select a professional author photo. This helps readers connect with you as the author and adds credibility to your work.
9. Page Requirements: Be aware of any minimum page requirements for your target age group. Some platforms may have specific guidelines for different genres or age categories.
10. Error Resolution: Be prepared to address any errors or issues that arise during the publishing process. This may include formatting errors, quality concerns, or metadata inaccuracies.

By following this checklist and paying attention to each detail, you can ensure a smooth and successful self-publishing experience. With careful planning and preparation, you'll be well on your way to seeing your book in the hands of eager readers.

Once you've thoroughly checked off each item on the checklist, you're on the brink of bringing your book to life. It's essential to approach the self-publishing journey with meticulous attention to detail and unwavering dedication. Your manuscript represents the culmination of your creativity and hard work, so ensuring it's polished and error-free is paramount. Likewise, investing in high-quality illustrations and a captivating book cover is crucial for grabbing the attention of potential readers and making a lasting impression.

Choosing the right publishing platform is another critical decision. While platforms like Amazon offer convenience and reach, others like IngramSpark may provide more flexibility and distribution options. Understanding the formatting requirements and nuances of each platform ensures your book meets their standards and reaches its intended audience effectively.

Crafting a compelling book description that succinctly captures the essence of your story is essential for generating interest and driving sales. Similarly, your author bio serves as a personal connection point for readers, allowing them to learn more about the person behind the book.

Navigating the self-publishing landscape may come with its challenges, such as encountering errors or facing rejection due to quality issues. However, with perseverance and a commitment to excellence, you can overcome these obstacles and achieve your publishing goals.

As you embark on this journey, remember to celebrate each milestone and embrace the learning opportunities along the way. Self-publishing offers unparalleled creative freedom and the chance to share your story with the world on your terms. By following the checklist and approaching the process with passion and determination, you're well-equipped to navigate the exciting world of self-publishing and bring your book to fruition.

Your Manuscript should have some or all of the following:

Each of these elements plays a crucial role in providing information, setting the tone, and engaging readers with your children's book manuscript. Once you've prepared and checked off each item, your manuscript will be well-structured and ready for publication.

- Copyright Page
- Dedication Page
- Title Page
- Acknowledgement Page (optional)
- Other Titles Page (optional)
- Introduction
- Chapters
- Meet the Author Page (optional)

Choosing A Book Release Date

Take a meticulous approach to publishing your book. Rushing the process can lead to various issues and headaches down the line, including errors in formatting, incomplete content, or missed opportunities for promotion. By ensuring your manuscript is fully complete and polished before uploading it for publication, you're setting yourself up for a smoother and more successful launch.

Choosing a book release date is a critical decision that requires careful consideration. It's wise to select a publication date that aligns with your marketing and promotional plans, allowing you ample time to generate buzz and build anticipation among your target audience. Additionally, scheduling your release date well in advance gives you the opportunity to coordinate any promotional activities, such as book signings, interviews, or social media campaigns, to maximize visibility and engagement.

When you upload your book for publication, it's essential to understand that it may take some time for it to go live on retail platforms. While the process typically takes up to 72 hours, unforeseen delays can occur, so it's best to plan accordingly. By selecting a publication date that aligns with your upload date, you ensure that your book is available for purchase on the day you intend to launch it to the public.

Ultimately, taking a methodical approach to publishing, from manuscript preparation to release date selection, minimizes the risk of encountering problems and maximizes your chances of a successful book launch. By adhering to your standards of quality and completeness, you set yourself up for a rewarding publishing experience and increase the likelihood of your book resonating with readers.

HERE'S A MORE DETAILED expansion on the importance of selecting the right book release date and the benefits of ensuring your manuscript is fully ready before publication:

1. Strategic Release Date Selection: Your book release date sets the tone for your entire launch strategy. By carefully choosing a date that aligns with your marketing efforts, you can maximize exposure and generate excitement among your audience. Consider factors such as seasonal trends, relevant events or holidays, and potential competition from other book releases when selecting your date.
2. Preparation for Promotional Activities: A well-planned release date gives you time to prepare and execute promotional activities effectively. Whether it's organizing book signings, reaching out to influencers for reviews, or launching advertising campaigns, having a clear timeline allows you to coordinate these efforts for maximum impact.
3. Avoiding Last-Minute Rush: Rushing to publish your book without ensuring it's fully ready can lead to stress and mistakes. By taking the time to thoroughly review and finalize your manuscript before uploading it for publication, you reduce the risk of encountering issues that could delay your release or compromise the quality of your book.
4. Maintaining Professionalism: Publishing a book is a significant achievement, and you want to present your work in the best possible light. Releasing a polished, complete manuscript demonstrates professionalism and respect for your readers. It also helps build trust and credibility as an author, encouraging readers to engage with your future works.
5. Optimizing Launch Impact: A well-prepared, strategically timed release sets the stage for a successful launch. By ensuring your book is fully ready and coordinating your release date with your promotional efforts, you can generate momentum

and buzz around your book, increasing its visibility and potential for success.

I firmly believe taking the time to select the right release date and ensuring your manuscript is fully prepared before publication are crucial steps in the publishing process. By approaching your book launch with careful planning and attention to detail, you set yourself up for a smooth, successful release that resonates with readers and establishes your presence in the literary world.

I HAVE PROVIDED A FEW sample pages to help you along the way. I feel that visual examples aid a great deal.

COPYRIGHT PAGE SAMPLE:

Copyright © 2024 by [Your Name]

All rights reserved. No part of this publication may be reproduced, distributed, or transmitted in any form or by any means, including photocopying, recording, or other electronic or mechanical methods, without the prior written permission of the publisher, except in the case of brief quotations embodied in critical reviews and certain other noncommercial uses permitted by copyright law.

For permissions requests, write to the publisher at:

Anywhere Press

[Publisher's Address]

[City, State, ZIP]

www.anywherepress.com

ISBN: 978-1-234567-89-0(sample number)

Printed in the United States of America

Cover design by [Cover Designer Name]

Illustrations by [Illustrations Designer Name]Illustrator Name]

Sample Dedication Page:

Dedication

To my loving family,
who have always encouraged my creativity
and supported my dreams.

FEEL FREE TO PERSONALIZE the dedication page with your own message to the intended recipient(s) of your dedication.

Sample Title Page:

The Adorable Teddy Bear
and the Fire Engine
Written by Felicity Whoever

Other Titles Page Example:

OTHER TITLES BY THIS Author

ELEPHANTS AND FIREFLIES

Rita and the Chocolate Bar
Mary and the Candy Apple
Morgan the Monkey

Meet the Author Page Example:

Provide Photo at the top of the page(optional)

MEET THE AUTHOR

Hello, young readers!

My name is John Doe, and I'm thrilled to be the author of [Book Title]. Writing stories for children is my passion, and I hope that you enjoy reading this book as much as I enjoyed writing it for you.

Growing up, I was always drawn to the magical worlds and colorful characters found in books. From adventurous journeys to heartwarming tales, each story I read sparked my imagination and inspired me to create my own. Now, as an author, I have the opportunity to share my imagination with you through the pages of [Book Title].

When I'm not writing, you can often find me exploring the great outdoors, playing with my pets, or trying out new recipes in the kitchen. I believe that life is an adventure waiting to be discovered, and I hope that my stories ignite a sense of curiosity and wonder in you.

Thank you for joining me on this journey, and I look forward to sharing many more adventures with you in the future!

Happy reading!

John Doe

Feel free to customize this "Meet the Author" page with your own personal details, interests, and writing style. It's an opportunity to connect with your young readers and share a bit about yourself and your love for storytelling.

Book Cover Design

Hiring a professional book cover designer can indeed be a wise investment, especially if you're aiming for a cover that stands out, captures attention, and effectively communicates the essence of your book. The typical price range for hiring a book cover designer varies depending on factors such as the designer's experience, the complexity of the design, and whether illustrations or custom artwork are involved.

In general, you can expect to pay anywhere from $200 to $1500 or more for a professionally designed book cover. This price may include initial consultations, concept development, revisions, and final file delivery. Some designers may also offer additional services such as formatting for different platforms or creating promotional materials.

While hiring a professional designer can be beneficial, it's also empowering to learn how to create your own book covers. There are numerous online resources, tutorials, and design software available that can help you develop your design skills. By learning to DIY your book covers, you gain creative control, save on costs, and have the flexibility to experiment with different concepts until you achieve the desired result.

Ultimately, whether you choose to hire a professional book cover designer or create your own cover, the key is to prioritize quality, creativity, and alignment with your book's content and target audience. A compelling book cover is an essential marketing tool that can make a significant difference in attracting readers and setting your book apart in a competitive market.

Continuing to explore the options for book cover design, it's important to recognize the value that professional designers bring to the table. They have the expertise to create visually stunning covers that not only look great but also effectively communicate the tone and genre of your book. Professional designers also have access to resources such as high-quality images, fonts, and design software, which can elevate the overall look of your cover.

However, if you're inclined toward a hands-on approach and enjoy the challenge of learning new skills, DIY book cover design can be a rewarding endeavor. With the abundance of online tutorials, design software, and stock image libraries available, aspiring authors have more opportunities than ever to create professional-looking covers from the comfort of their own homes. By investing time and effort into learning design principles and experimenting with different concepts, you can develop the skills needed to produce eye-catching covers that captivate your audience.

Moreover, DIY book cover design allows for greater flexibility and creative control. You can tailor the design to perfectly match your vision for the book and make adjustments as needed throughout the process. Additionally, by mastering the art of cover design, you gain valuable skills that can be applied to future projects, saving you time and money in the long run.

Whether you choose to hire a professional designer or embark on a DIY journey, the most important thing is to prioritize the quality and effectiveness of your book cover. It's the first impression readers will have of your book, so make it count by creating a cover that resonates with your audience and entices them to explore what lies within.

Social Media

In today's digital landscape, I firmly believe that leveraging social media is indispensable for authors seeking to maximize the visibility of their books. As both an author and the owner of my own imprint or publishing house, I've observed that many mainstream publishing houses are adopting similar strategies. The accessibility of technology and the prevalence of metadata in the digital age have leveled the playing field, allowing authors of all backgrounds to compete for attention in the market.

Having embarked on my journey as an author and publisher, I've witnessed firsthand the power of social media in reaching and engaging with readers. Platforms like Instagram, Twitter, and Facebook offer invaluable opportunities to connect with audiences, share updates about my books, and foster a sense of community among readers. These channels provide a direct line of communication with my audience, enabling me to receive feedback, answer questions, and cultivate relationships that extend beyond the pages of my books.

Despite having published over 40 books, I recognize that there is always more to learn in this ever-evolving industry. While I've honed my expertise in various aspects of publishing, I remain humble and open to new insights and strategies. As I continue to navigate the dynamic landscape of publishing, I approach each day with the mindset of a perpetual student, eager to absorb knowledge, refine my skills, and adapt to emerging trends.

With my children's books gaining traction and finding success, I'm encouraged by the potential that social media holds for expanding their reach even further. By staying proactive, innovative, and engaged with my audience online, I'm confident that I can continue to grow as both an author and a publisher, bringing my stories to an ever-widening audience and making a meaningful impact in the literary world.

Harnessing the power of social media has been instrumental in propelling my children's books forward and fostering connections with readers. Through strategic use of platforms like Instagram and Twitter, I've been able to share glimpses into the creative process, offer behind-the-scenes insights, and build anticipation for upcoming releases. Engaging with parents, educators, and young readers directly on these platforms has provided invaluable feedback and sparked meaningful conversations about the themes and messages conveyed in my books.

As I navigate this journey of authorship and publishing, I remain committed to embracing the opportunities afforded by social media while also recognizing the importance of continuous learning and growth. Each interaction, whether positive or constructive, serves as a stepping stone toward refining my craft and honing my approach to storytelling. By staying attuned to the needs and interests of my audience, I strive to create books that resonate deeply and leave a lasting impression.

Looking ahead, I am excited by the possibilities that social media presents for expanding my reach and amplifying the impact of my books. By embracing innovation, staying adaptable, and remaining steadfast in my dedication to creating meaningful content, I am confident that I can continue to thrive in an increasingly digital world. With social media as my ally, I am poised to embark on the next chapter of my journey with optimism, enthusiasm, and a steadfast commitment to sharing stories that inspire, educate, and delight readers of all ages.

Book Signing and Launch

As I explore different avenues for celebrating my book's completion and sharing it with the world, I'm reminded that success in the publishing industry often requires resilience and creativity. While securing a book signing with a major retailer like Books-A-Million may present challenges, I refuse to let setbacks dampen my enthusiasm. Instead, I'm inspired to think outside the box and consider alternative venues where I can connect with readers and celebrate my achievement.

Hosting a book launch at a local library, community center, or even my own home offers intimate settings that foster meaningful interactions with attendees. These venues provide the flexibility to personalize the event and create a memorable experience for everyone involved. Additionally, reaching out to local book clubs, schools, or organizations allows me to tap into existing communities and expand my reach beyond traditional retail channels.

Ordering author copies from my publishing platform not only enables me to showcase my book at events but also opens up opportunities for selling directly to readers. By leveraging social media, word-of-mouth marketing, and online platforms like Amazon and Etsy, I can reach a wider audience and drive sales while maintaining control over my distribution channels.

Despite the challenges and uncertainties inherent in the publishing journey, I remain optimistic and determined to share my story with the world. Whether through book signings, community events, or online promotions, I'm committed to celebrating my accomplishment and connecting with readers who will find joy and inspiration in my work. With perseverance and creativity, I believe that every setback is an opportunity for growth and every obstacle is a chance to shine.

As I continue to work through the process of book promotion and celebration, I'm reminded of the importance of perseverance and adaptability. While setbacks with securing book signings at major retailers like Books-A-Million may be discouraging, they serve as valuable learning experiences. Rather than viewing them as roadblocks, I see them as opportunities to explore new avenues for engagement and connection with readers.

One alternative approach I'm considering is organizing virtual events and online book launches. With the rise of digital platforms and the increasing accessibility of technology, virtual events offer a convenient and inclusive way to reach audiences worldwide. Through webinars, live streams, and social media events, I can engage with readers from the comfort of their own homes, breaking down geographical barriers and expanding my reach beyond traditional brick-and-mortar settings.

Additionally, collaborating with local businesses, bookstores, or literary organizations can provide mutually beneficial opportunities for promotion and exposure. By partnering with like-minded individuals or groups, I can leverage their existing networks and resources to amplify the visibility of my book and attract a broader audience.

Ultimately, while the journey of book promotion may have its challenges, it's also filled with moments of creativity, connection, and celebration. By embracing flexibility and embracing new possibilities, I'm confident that I can navigate the ever-changing landscape of publishing with resilience and enthusiasm. With each step forward, I'm one step closer to sharing my story with the world and making a meaningful impact in the lives of readers everywhere.

Now, as I mentioned earlier, when it comes to sharing your book with the world, social media is your best friend. It's an essential tool for connecting with readers and building buzz around your book. Think of it as your virtual book launch platform, where you can share sneak peeks, behind-the-scenes stories, and updates on your progress. Don't be afraid to get creative and engage with your audience—it's all about building a community around your book.

Also, Barnes & Noble is a popular option for book signings as well, but don't forget about other venues like local libraries, community centers, or even your own home. And if you're having trouble securing a signing with a big retailer, don't sweat it! There are plenty of other opportunities out there, like virtual events or collaborations with local businesses.

When it comes to selling your book, ordering author copies from your publishing platform is key. This allows you to showcase your book at events and sell directly to readers, giving you more control over your distribution channels. And don't forget about online platforms like Amazon and Etsy—they're great for reaching a wider audience and driving sales.

SOCIAL MEDIA STRATEGY: Social media is your stage for connecting with readers and building excitement around your book. Consistency and authenticity are key. Let's develop a content calendar to ensure you're regularly engaging with your audience. Consider sharing snippets of your writing process, hosting Q&A sessions, or even running giveaways to generate buzz. Remember, it's all about building genuine connections, so be sure to respond to comments and messages thoughtfully.

Book Signings and Events: While securing a book signing with a major retailer is a fantastic opportunity, it's not the only path to success. Let's explore a variety of venues for events, such as local bookstores, coffee shops, or community centers. Virtual events are also a convenient way to connect with readers from around the world. Persistence is key here—sometimes it takes multiple inquiries or follow-ups to secure an event, but don't let that discourage you.

Overcoming Setbacks: Setbacks are a natural part of the publishing journey, but they shouldn't derail your dreams. View them as learning opportunities and stay flexible in your approach. If one door closes, remember that there are always other avenues to explore. Reflect on your accomplishments thus far and the progress you've made. You've come a long way, and you're capable of overcoming any challenges that come your way.

Direct Sales and Online Platforms: Direct sales can be a powerful way to connect with readers and maximize your earnings. Consider setting up an online store on your website or utilizing platforms like Amazon's Kindle Direct Publishing for ebooks and print-on-demand copies. Offering personalized signed copies can also incentivize readers to purchase directly from you. Keep exploring new opportunities and approaches, and remember that each step brings you closer to achieving your goals as an author.

By looking into these areas and approaching them with creativity, perseverance, and an open mind, you'll gain a comprehensive understanding of the various avenues available for promoting your book and connecting with readers. Embrace each opportunity as a chance to grow and learn, knowing that you're one step closer to achieving your dreams as an author. Keep pushing forward, and never lose sight of your passion for storytelling. You've got this!

The Cost of Publishing Your Book

Let's dive into the costs associated with writing a book. It's crucial to approach this aspect with caution, as expenses can quickly add up if not managed wisely. As your coach, I want to ensure you have a clear understanding of what to expect and how to navigate the financial aspects of the writing process.

First and foremost, one of the most significant expenses you may encounter is hiring professional services such as editors, cover designers, and formatting specialists. While these services are essential for producing a high-quality book, they can be costly. It's essential to budget accordingly and do thorough research to find reputable professionals whose rates align with your budget.

Additionally, there are costs associated with research materials, software, and marketing efforts. Depending on the genre, if you ever want to publish outside of being a children's author and subject matter of your book, you may need to invest in books, courses, or subscriptions to access relevant information and resources. Similarly, investing in marketing and promotional activities is crucial for getting your book noticed, whether it's through advertising, book launches, or author events.

As I touched on earlier, self-publishing also comes with its own set of expenses, including ISBNs, printing costs, and distribution fees. While self-publishing offers greater control and potential for higher royalties, it's essential to carefully consider these expenses and weigh them against the benefits.

Ultimately, the key to managing costs effectively is careful planning and budgeting. Take the time to research and compare prices for services and materials, and prioritize your spending based on what will have the most significant impact on the quality and success of your book. Remember that investing in your book is an investment in your future as an author, and with thoughtful planning, you can ensure that your financial resources are put to good use in bringing your vision to life. As your coach, I'm here to support you every step of the way and help you navigate the financial aspects of your writing journey.

Furthermore, it's crucial to recognize that the costs associated with writing a book can vary widely depending on factors such as the length and complexity of the manuscript, the genre, and your individual preferences and goals as an author. For example, a non-fiction book that requires extensive research and interviews may incur higher expenses than a work of fiction set in a fictional world. Similarly, if you choose to pursue traditional publishing, you may not incur upfront costs for editing and cover design, but you may face additional expenses related to marketing and promotion.

As your coach, I encourage you to approach the financial aspect of writing with a clear understanding of your budget and priorities. Take the time to assess your resources and determine how much you're willing and able to invest in your book project. Consider seeking advice from other authors or industry professionals who have experience navigating the financial aspects of writing and publishing.

It's also important to keep in mind that while investing in professional services and marketing efforts can enhance the quality and visibility of your book, there are also cost-effective strategies you can employ. For example, you may choose to trade services with other authors or utilize free or low-cost marketing platforms such as social media and book promotion websites.

Ultimately, the key is to strike a balance between investing in your book's success and managing your expenses responsibly. By approaching the financial aspect of writing with foresight and careful planning, you can maximize the impact of your investment and increase your chances of achieving your goals as an author. Remember, writing a book is a journey, and with thoughtful consideration and strategic decision-making, you can navigate the financial landscape with confidence and success.

Benefits of Becoming a Children's Author

Becoming a children's author is an incredibly rewarding journey that not only allows you to share your creativity and imagination with young readers but also makes a meaningful contribution to the world. As a children's author, you have the opportunity to create stories that inspire, educate, and entertain, shaping the minds and hearts of future generations. Here are some compelling reasons to embark on the path of becoming a children's author and bring your book to life.

First and foremost, writing a children's book allows you to make a lasting impact on the lives of young readers. Children's literature has the power to spark curiosity, ignite imagination, and instill valuable life lessons in a way that resonates deeply with young minds. By crafting stories that captivate and inspire, you have the opportunity to shape the way children see themselves, others, and the world around them.

Moreover, becoming a children's author offers a unique platform to address important issues and promote diversity, inclusion, and empathy. Through your storytelling, you can introduce children to characters from diverse backgrounds, cultures, and experiences, fostering understanding and empathy from an early age. By weaving themes of kindness, resilience, and acceptance into your narratives, you can empower young readers to navigate the complexities of the world with compassion and empathy.

Additionally, writing a children's book allows you to tap into your own creativity and imagination in a way that is both fulfilling and inspiring. Whether you're crafting fantastical adventures, heartwarming tales, or educational stories, the process of writing allows you to explore new worlds, characters, and ideas, stretching your creative muscles and expanding your horizons as an author.

Furthermore, becoming a published children's author opens up a world of opportunities for personal and professional growth. From book signings and author events to school visits and literary festivals, you have the chance to connect with readers, educators, and fellow authors, building a supportive community around your work. The sense of accomplishment and fulfillment that comes from seeing your book in the hands of young readers is truly unparalleled.

For me, becoming a children's author is a deeply rewarding journey that allows you to make a meaningful contribution to the world while fulfilling your own creative potential. By sharing your stories with young readers, you have the power to inspire, educate, and empower the next generation, leaving a lasting legacy that will continue to resonate for years to come. So why wait? Take the leap and bring your book to life—you have the power to make a difference in the lives of children everywhere.

It is wonderful that you have a passion for children's books and that you still maintain that magical and youthful perspective. Let's delve deeper into why becoming a children's author is not only fun but also incredibly rewarding for you.

As a children's author, you have the unique opportunity to tap into your inner child and explore the limitless boundaries of imagination. Writing and illustrating children's books allow you to revisit that sense of wonder and curiosity that defines childhood. Whether you're crafting whimsical characters, dreamy landscapes, or enchanting adventures, you have the freedom to let your imagination run wild and create stories that transport young readers to magical worlds beyond their wildest dreams.

From my view, writing for children allows you to connect with your audience on a deeply personal level. Children are naturally drawn to stories that resonate with their experiences, emotions, and aspirations. By infusing your writing with authenticity, empathy, and a touch of whimsy, you can create stories that speak directly to the hearts of young readers, fostering a sense of connection and belonging that is truly magical.

In addition to the joy of writing and illustrating, becoming a children's author offers a sense of fulfillment and purpose that goes beyond creative expression. Knowing that your books have the power to inspire, educate, and entertain young minds is incredibly rewarding. Whether you're teaching valuable life lessons, sparking curiosity about the world, or simply bringing joy and laughter to children's lives, the impact of your work is immeasurable.

Furthermore, becoming a children's author allows you to leave a lasting legacy that extends far beyond the pages of your books. The stories you create have the potential to shape the way children see themselves, others, and the world around them, leaving a positive and lasting impact on their lives. By sharing your creativity, wisdom, and passion for storytelling, you have the power to inspire the next generation of readers, writers, and dreamers.

I sincerely believe, becoming a children's author is not just about writing and illustrating books—it's about embracing your inner child, sharing your love of storytelling, and making a positive difference in the lives of young readers. By embracing your passion for children's books and infusing your work with creativity, authenticity, and wonder, you can create stories that capture the hearts and imaginations of children everywhere. So keep writing, keep dreaming, and keep sharing your magic with the world—you have the power to make childhood a little more enchanting for generations to come.

Marketing Your Book

Absolutely, let's look into smart and cost-effective ways to market your book in today's digital age, especially without the backing of a traditional publisher:

In today's digital landscape, marketing your book without the support of a traditional publisher is not only feasible but can also be incredibly effective with the right strategies in place. One of the most powerful tools at your disposal is social media. Platforms like Facebook, Instagram, Twitter, and TikTok offer unparalleled opportunities to connect with your target audience, build a following, and generate buzz around your book—all without breaking the bank.

First and foremost, it's essential to establish a strong online presence by creating dedicated author profiles on social media. These profiles should reflect your brand and personality and serve as hubs for engaging with your audience and sharing updates about your book. Regularly post content that resonates with your target audience, such as behind-the-scenes glimpses into your writing process, sneak peeks of upcoming projects, or engaging discussions related to your book's themes.

Utilizing social media features like live videos, stories, and interactive polls can help you foster deeper connections with your audience and keep them engaged. Encourage your followers to participate by asking questions, sharing their thoughts and experiences, and inviting them to be part of your journey as an author. Remember, authenticity and genuine engagement are key to building a loyal and enthusiastic fan base.

Another cost-effective way to market your book is by leveraging the power of book bloggers, bookstagrammers, and booktubers. These influencers have dedicated followings of book enthusiasts who trust their recommendations and opinions. Reach out to influencers in your genre and offer them free copies of your book in exchange for honest reviews, shoutouts, or features on their platforms. Their endorsement can help boost visibility and credibility for your book among their followers.

Additionally, don't underestimate the value of online communities and forums dedicated to literature and writing. Platforms like Goodreads, Reddit, and online book clubs offer opportunities to connect with readers who are actively seeking recommendations and discussions about books. Participate in these communities by sharing insights, engaging in conversations, and promoting your book in a way that adds value to the community rather than coming across as overly promotional.

Email marketing is another powerful tool for reaching your audience directly and promoting your book effectively. Build an email list of subscribers who have expressed interest in your work, whether through your website, social media, or events. Send out regular newsletters with updates about your book, exclusive content, behind-the-scenes insights, and special offers to keep your audience engaged and excited about your work.

So, consider partnering with other authors, bloggers, or organizations in your niche to cross-promote each other's work. Collaborative marketing efforts, such as joint giveaways, blog tours, or social media shoutouts, can help you reach new audiences and expand your network within the literary community.

Finally, don't underestimate the power of traditional marketing tactics such as press releases, book signings, and local events. While these strategies may require some investment upfront, they can be highly effective in generating local buzz and building relationships with readers, booksellers, and community organizations.

Remember, marketing your book without the backing of a traditional publisher requires creativity, persistence, and a strategic approach. By leveraging the power of social media, influencer partnerships, online communities, email marketing, and traditional tactics, you can effectively promote your book, connect with your target audience, and achieve your goals as an author—all while staying within your budget. Remember, building a successful author platform takes time and effort, but with the right strategies and mindset, you can make a meaningful impact and attract readers to your book.

Exploring YouTube as a marketing tool for your book can open up a world of possibilities and reach a broader audience. Here's how you can utilize YouTube effectively to promote your book and engage with potential readers:

YouTube offers a diverse range of opportunities for authors to showcase their work, connect with readers, and build a loyal fan base. One of the most effective ways to leverage YouTube for book marketing is by creating engaging and informative content that resonates with your target audience. Consider starting your own YouTube channel dedicated to topics related to your book, such as writing tips, author interviews, book reviews, and behind-the-scenes insights into your writing process.

By providing valuable content that appeals to your audience's interests and preferences, you can attract subscribers and establish yourself as an authority in your niche.

In addition to creating original content, you can also explore collaboration opportunities with other YouTubers in your genre or niche. Partnering with influencers, booktubers, or writing vloggers who have a dedicated following of book enthusiasts can help you reach a larger audience and gain exposure for your book. Consider reaching out to YouTubers who create content related to your book's genre or themes and propose collaborative projects such as guest appearances, joint videos, or cross-promotion efforts. Their endorsement and support can help increase visibility and generate excitement for your book among their subscribers.

Another effective strategy for utilizing YouTube as a book marketing tool is by creating book trailers or promotional videos to showcase your book in a visually compelling way. A well-crafted book trailer can capture the essence of your story, evoke emotion, and pique the interest of potential readers. Consider hiring a professional videographer or utilizing DIY video editing tools to create a visually stunning and engaging trailer that highlights the key elements of your book, such as its plot, characters, and themes. Once created, you can share your book trailer on your YouTube channel, social media platforms, author website, and other online channels to attract attention and drive book sales.

Furthermore, YouTube offers a wealth of tutorials, guides, and resources that can help authors learn about book marketing strategies, self-publishing techniques, and promotional tactics. By tapping into the wealth of knowledge available on YouTube, you can gain valuable insights and practical tips to enhance your book marketing efforts and navigate the publishing journey with confidence. Consider subscribing to channels dedicated to topics such as self-publishing, book promotion, and author entrepreneurship to stay informed about the latest trends and developments in the industry. Additionally, you can explore playlists, webinars, and online courses offered by experienced authors, publishing professionals, and marketing experts to further expand your knowledge and skills.

So basically, YouTube offers authors a powerful platform to showcase their work, connect with readers, and promote their books effectively. By creating engaging content, collaborating with influencers, creating book trailers, and leveraging the wealth of resources available on YouTube, you can enhance your book marketing efforts and reach a wider audience. Whether you're just starting out or looking to expand your author platform, YouTube provides endless opportunities to connect with readers, build your brand, and achieve your goals as an author. So don't hesitate to explore the possibilities and harness the power of YouTube to elevate your book marketing strategy.

Professional Avenues And Monetization

Let's explore the professional opportunities and avenues for monetization that becoming a children's author can open up for you:

Becoming a children's author offers a multitude of professional opportunities and avenues for monetization that extend far beyond book sales. Here are some ways your book can benefit you professionally and how you can leverage your status as a children's author to generate income and establish yourself as a credible voice in your field.

First and foremost, publishing a children's book can elevate your professional status and enhance your credibility as an expert in your niche. Whether you're an educator, a parent, or a passionate storyteller, having a published book to your name demonstrates your expertise, creativity, and dedication to your craft. This can open doors to speaking engagements, teaching opportunities, and consulting gigs where you can share your knowledge and insights with others in your field.

In addition to traditional book sales, there are numerous ways to monetize your children's book and generate passive income over time. One option is to explore foreign rights sales, where you license the translation and publication rights of your book to publishers in other countries. This allows you to reach new markets and readerships while earning royalties from sales abroad. Similarly, audiobook rights can be a lucrative source of income, especially as the popularity of audio storytelling continues to rise. Consider partnering with a narrator or recording your own audiobook to make your story accessible to listeners of all ages.

Another way to monetize your children's book is by creating related merchandise and products inspired by your story. From plush toys and puzzles to clothing and accessories, the possibilities are endless. By leveraging your book's characters, themes, and artwork, you can develop a range of merchandise that appeals to your audience and enhances their engagement with your story. Consider partnering with a licensing agency or exploring print-on-demand services to bring your merchandise ideas to life without the need for large upfront investments.

Furthermore, your children's book can serve as a springboard for launching additional products, services, or ventures related to your brand and expertise. For example, you could offer online courses or workshops on topics such as storytelling, creativity, or literacy, leveraging your book's themes and messages to provide value to your audience. Alternatively, you could develop educational resources, activity books, or curriculum materials that complement your book and appeal to teachers, parents, and educators.

Additionally, becoming a children's author opens up opportunities for collaboration and partnership with other professionals in the publishing industry. Consider networking with illustrators, editors, agents, and publishers who share your passion for children's literature and exploring collaborative projects such as anthologies, series, or joint ventures. By pooling your talents and resources, you can create innovative and impactful storytelling experiences that resonate with readers and elevate your profile within the industry.

How awesome that, becoming a children's author offers numerous professional opportunities and avenues for monetization that extend far beyond book sales. From foreign rights sales and audiobooks to merchandise, courses, and collaborations, there are countless ways to leverage your book and establish yourself as a credible voice in your field. By thinking creatively, networking strategically, and exploring new possibilities, you can turn your passion for storytelling into a rewarding and sustainable career as a children's author.

Additionally, as a children's author, you have the opportunity to leverage your expertise and experience to offer valuable services and consultations to others in your field. For example, you could provide manuscript evaluations, editing services, or writing coaching to aspiring authors looking to hone their craft and bring their own stories to life. Your firsthand experience in navigating the publishing process, from concept to publication, gives you unique insights and perspectives that can be immensely valuable to others seeking guidance and support on their writing journey.

Furthermore, your status as a published children's author can open doors to speaking engagements, workshops, and author visits at schools, libraries, and literary events. Sharing your passion for storytelling and inspiring young minds through readings, interactive sessions, and discussions can be incredibly rewarding both personally and professionally. Not only does it provide an opportunity to connect with your audience on a deeper level, but it also helps to promote your book and expand your reach within the community.

Moreover, becoming a children's author affords you the opportunity to build a personal brand and establish yourself as a thought leader in your niche. By consistently sharing valuable content, insights, and expertise through your website, blog, social media channels, and other platforms, you can position yourself as a credible voice in the children's literature community. This, in turn, can lead to opportunities for media features, guest appearances, and collaborations with other influencers and organizations seeking your unique perspective and expertise.

In terms of monetization, there are also opportunities to explore affiliate marketing and sponsorship deals related to your book and brand. By partnering with relevant companies, brands, or products that align with your book's themes and audience, you can earn commissions or fees for promoting their products or services to your audience. For example, if your book focuses on outdoor adventures, you could partner with outdoor gear companies or travel agencies to promote their products or services to your readers.

Additionally, don't overlook the potential for passive income streams such as licensing deals, syndication rights, and reprint opportunities for your book. By strategically licensing your book's rights to other publishers, media outlets, or platforms, you can generate ongoing royalties and royalties from secondary sales and adaptations of your work. This can include everything from film and television adaptations to merchandise, stage productions, and digital media formats.

In conclusion, becoming a children's author opens up a world of professional opportunities and avenues for monetization beyond traditional book sales. By leveraging your expertise, creativity, and brand, you can offer valuable services, engage with audiences, and explore new revenue streams that enhance your career and elevate your impact as an author. With strategic planning, networking, and creativity, you can build a sustainable and fulfilling career as a children's author while making a meaningful difference in the lives of young readers everywhere.

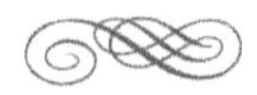

GIVING BACK

Giving back as an author is a wonderful way to make a positive impact on your community and inspire young readers. Here's how children's book authors can give back and engage with schools, libraries, and other organizations:

One of the most rewarding ways to give back as a children's book author is by reading to schools, libraries, and community organizations. Reading aloud to children not only promotes literacy and a love of books but also provides them with valuable opportunities to engage with authors and explore new worlds through storytelling. Consider reaching out to local schools, libraries, and literacy organizations to offer to read from your book and share your passion for storytelling with young audiences. Whether it's a virtual reading or an in-person visit, these events can leave a lasting impression on children and inspire them to become lifelong readers and writers.

In addition to reading to children, authors can also donate copies of their books to schools, libraries, and underprivileged communities to ensure that all children have access to quality literature. By partnering with organizations that support literacy initiatives, such as book drives, reading programs, or literacy nonprofits, authors can help to make a positive impact on children's education and inspire a love of reading in children who may not have access to books otherwise. Consider donating books to organizations that serve children in need, such as homeless shelters, foster care agencies, or hospitals, to bring joy and comfort to children facing difficult circumstances.

Furthermore, authors can use their books as a platform to raise awareness and support for important causes and social issues that are meaningful to them. Whether it's promoting diversity and inclusion, environmental conservation, or social justice, authors can leverage their storytelling skills to spark conversations, inspire action, and effect positive change in their communities and beyond. Consider partnering with advocacy organizations, nonprofits, or community groups to raise funds, awareness, or support for causes that align with the themes of your book.

Moreover, authors can host special events, workshops, or creative activities for children to further engage with their books and foster a sense of creativity and imagination. From interactive storytelling sessions and book-themed crafts to writing workshops and author Q&A sessions, there are countless ways to create meaningful experiences for young readers and inspire them to explore their own creativity and storytelling abilities. Consider hosting virtual events or partnering with local venues to host in-person events that bring children and families together to celebrate the joy of reading and storytelling.

I think that giving back as a children's book author is a meaningful way to make a positive impact on your community and inspire young readers to discover the magic of books and storytelling. Whether it's reading to children, donating books to schools and libraries, supporting literacy initiatives, raising awareness for important causes, or hosting special events and workshops, authors have endless opportunities to give back and make a difference in the lives of children everywhere. By sharing their passion for storytelling and promoting literacy, authors can help to create a brighter future for generations to come.

Philanthropy is a powerful force for positive change, and when authors give back, it creates a ripple effect of generosity and goodwill in their communities and beyond. Let's delve deeper into the impact of philanthropy in the context of children's book authors:

First and foremost, giving back as an author allows you to directly contribute to the well-being and development of children in your community. By donating books, reading to children, and hosting educational events, you provide valuable opportunities for children to engage with literature, expand their imaginations, and develop essential literacy skills that will serve them throughout their lives. These experiences not only foster a love of reading but also inspire children to explore new ideas, broaden their perspectives, and pursue their passions.

Philanthropy allows authors to use their platform and influence to address important social issues and advocate for positive change. By aligning their books and activities with causes they care about, authors can raise awareness, inspire action, and mobilize their readers to make a difference in the world. Whether it's promoting diversity and inclusion, environmental stewardship, or social justice, authors have the power to spark meaningful conversations and drive meaningful impact through their storytelling and advocacy efforts.

Giving back as an author creates a sense of community and connection that enriches both the giver and the recipient. When authors engage with schools, libraries, and community organizations, they have the opportunity to build meaningful relationships with educators, librarians, families, and children who share their love of books and storytelling. These connections foster a sense of belonging and collaboration that strengthens the fabric of the community and creates lasting bonds that transcend the pages of a book.

Additionally, philanthropy provides authors with a sense of purpose and fulfillment that goes beyond commercial success. Knowing that their books are making a positive impact on the lives of children and families brings a sense of joy and satisfaction that money alone cannot buy. Whether it's seeing the smiles on children's faces as they listen to a story or receiving heartfelt thank-you notes from grateful educators and parents, authors who give back experience the true meaning of success and fulfillment in their work.

Philanthropy is a cornerstone of a thriving and compassionate society, and when authors give back, they play a vital role in shaping the future of their communities and the world. By donating books, advocating for important causes, and engaging with readers in meaningful ways, authors can inspire a new generation of changemakers and create a legacy of kindness, generosity, and empathy that will endure for generations to come. So let's continue to celebrate the power of philanthropy and the incredible impact it has on the lives of children, families, and communities everywhere.

You Can Do It

I am absolutely rooting for you! I believe wholeheartedly that you can do it—you can publish your children's book and share your story with the world. While the journey may seem daunting at times, with dedication, perseverance, and a clear vision, you can overcome any obstacles that stand in your way. Remember, every successful author started somewhere, and each step you take brings you closer to achieving your dreams. Whether you choose to pursue traditional publishing, self-publishing, or independent publishing, know that you have the power to bring your creative vision to life and make a positive impact on young readers' lives. So keep writing, keep revising, and keep believing in yourself, because your story deserves to be told and your voice deserves to be heard. With passion, patience, and persistence, you can turn your children's book dreams into reality, one word at a time.

As you embark on this journey, it's essential to stay focused on your goals and remain committed to the process, even when faced with challenges or setbacks along the way. Writing and publishing a children's book is a labor of love, requiring dedication, resilience, and a willingness to learn and grow as an author. Trust in your creativity and believe in the unique perspective and voice that you bring to your storytelling. Your experiences, insights, and imagination are what make your book truly special and deserving of publication.

Don't be afraid to seek support and guidance from fellow writers, mentors, and industry professionals who can offer valuable advice, encouragement, and feedback throughout your publishing journey. Building a network of peers and allies can provide you with the encouragement and resources you need to navigate the complexities of the publishing process and overcome any obstacles that may arise.

Additionally, take the time to research and educate yourself about the various publishing options available to you, from traditional publishing houses to self-publishing platforms and everything in between. Each path has its own advantages and considerations, so it's essential to weigh your options carefully and choose the approach that aligns best with your goals, preferences, and resources.

If you decide to pursue traditional publishing, be prepared to invest time and effort into crafting a compelling query letter, synopsis, and manuscript that will capture the attention of literary agents and editors. Remember to research prospective agents and publishers carefully, ensuring that they are a good fit for your book and that you understand their submission guidelines and requirements.

On the other hand, if you choose to self-publish or independently publish your book, embrace the opportunity to take control of the publishing process and bring your vision to life on your own terms. Invest in professional editing, design, and marketing services to ensure that your book meets industry standards and stands out in a crowded marketplace. And don't forget to leverage the power of digital and social media platforms to connect with readers and promote your book to a wide audience.

Above all, never lose sight of why you started writing in the first place—to share your story, inspire young minds, and make a positive impact on the world. Keep your passion and enthusiasm alive throughout the publishing process, and remember that every step forward, no matter how small, brings you closer to achieving your dreams. With determination, perseverance, and a belief in yourself and your work, you can publish your children's book and embark on a fulfilling and rewarding journey as an author. So take that first step, and let your imagination soar as you bring your book to life for readers of all ages to enjoy.

Epilogue:

As we reach the conclusion of "You Can Write a Children's Book: A Guide to Help You Publish," I hope you feel inspired, empowered, and ready to embark on your journey as a children's author. Writing and publishing a book is a remarkable achievement, and whether you're just starting out or have been dreaming of becoming an author for years, know that your voice and your story matter.

Remember, the path to publication may be filled with twists and turns, challenges and triumphs, but every step you take brings you closer to realizing your dreams. Whether you choose traditional publishing, self-publishing, or independent publishing, embrace the process with enthusiasm and determination. Surround yourself with a supportive community of fellow writers, mentors, and industry professionals who can offer guidance, encouragement, and invaluable insights along the way.

Above all, never lose sight of the magic and wonder of storytelling. Children's literature has the power to ignite imaginations, inspire curiosity, and spark a lifelong love of reading in young readers. As you share your stories with the world, know that you are making a difference in the lives of children everywhere, one page at a time.

So go forth, dear author, and let your creativity soar. Write with passion, purpose, and authenticity, and trust in the unique gifts and talents that you bring to the world of children's literature. May your journey be filled with joy, fulfillment, and endless adventures, and may your stories bring laughter, learning, and love to readers of all ages for generations to come.

Thank you for joining me on this incredible journey. May your writing dreams take flight, and may you always remember that you have the power to write the next chapter of your story. Happy writing!

Bibliography: Sources Cited

• "Secrets of a Successful Published Author" by Kim Ruff Moore (Ruff Moore Publishing)

• This book offers valuable insights and practical advice on the process of writing and publishing children's books. Drawing on her own experiences as an author and publisher, Kim Ruff Moore provides tips and strategies for success in both independent and traditional publishing.

Meet The Author

Kim Ruff Moore is a multifaceted artist whose talents have touched hearts across the globe. As a Stellar Award-winning singer-songwriter and national recording artist, Kim's voice carries messages of hope and inspiration.

Beyond her musical achievements, Kim has established herself as a prolific author with an impressive repertoire of 35 published books. Her works span various genres, from children's literature to insightful guides on finances and relationships. Kim's dedication to uplifting others is evident in the five-star ratings her books consistently receive.

A champion of literacy, Kim has created several beloved book series for children, including "Suzzie Moch," "Spence Seven," "Sergio the Studio Mouse," "Kirby the Koala," and "Harper Sharper," among others. Through imaginative storytelling, Kim instills valuable lessons and fosters creativity in young minds.

Kim's creative endeavors extend beyond the written word. She is a proud member of the duo group "The New Consolers," alongside her husband, Jeffrey Moore, who is a renowned music producer with roots in the legendary Sam Cooke band. Jeffrey's induction into the DooWap Hall of Fame in 2013 is a testament to his musical legacy.

Together, Kim and Jeffrey captivate audiences worldwide with their soul-stirring performances. Their shared passion for music and storytelling creates an unforgettable experience for listeners of all ages.

In addition to her artistic pursuits, Kim generously shares her literary platform at various functions and speaking engagements, inspiring others to pursue their passions and fulfill their potential.

Kim and Jeffrey's family life is equally enriching, with four children who undoubtedly inherit their parents' creativity and drive. Their son Spencer, also a writer, serves as the inspiration behind the acclaimed "Spence Seven" book series, continuing the family's legacy of storytelling and inspiration.

Through her music, writing, and advocacy, Kim Ruff Moore continues to make a profound impact, spreading joy and empowerment wherever her talents take her.

Milton Keynes UK
Ingram Content Group UK Ltd.
UKHW011505050524
442175UK00001B/32